SINGLE
MOTHERHOOD

SINGLE MOTHERHOOD

SECRETS OF SUCCESS AND BEYOND

CJ ROSE

PARTRIDGE

To order additional copies of this book, contact
Toll Free 800 101 2657 (Singapore)
Toll Free 1 800 81 7340 (Malaysia)
orders.singapore@partridgepublishing.com

www.partridgepublishing.com/singapore

CONTENTS

DEDICATION

This book is dedicated to all my family and friends for their love, devotion, understanding, endless support, and for being my pillars of strength during the difficult times.

To my beloved parents - without whom I would not be here.

To my treasured late maternal grandma – who cared me for as a child and showed me unconditional love. For your quiet guidance - your actions that spoke louder than your words has had a profound impact on me.

To my beloved children - your growth provides me with a constant source of joy and pride and who will eventually make this world a better place.

To my sister – who helped me get back on my feet. For the down payment of my first house after my divorce and the loan of her 13-year old car that got me from A to B.

To my divorce lawyer *LG* – for your encouragement and sound advice. For taking on my case despite my financial constraints, and for taking the trouble to come to Seremban to help me get my belongings when I finally made the choice to end my marriage.

To my best friend forever (BFF) *JW* – for your unconditional friendship. For just being there for me and listening without judging and providing me emotional support when I needed it most.

To my beloved *'Amazing Day'* thank you for always believing in me. Thank you for your true and unconditional love. I love you to the moon and back.

To my spiritual guru *ST* – for spiritual guidance and teaching me to meditate as a way of letting go of my past sufferings. He taught me the most important lesson - nothing here on earth is permanent.

To single mothers around the world that dream of becoming financially independent and rebuilding a happy, successful and rewarding life, but are too intimidated and scared to take that first step. It is my hope and dream that this book fills you with inspiration and hopes and might be that first step.

To my editor *FM* – for her patience, support, understanding, time and consultation as well as catching mistakes, suggesting ideas and making changes that may seem obvious in retrospection but that would never have otherwise occurred to me.

To my publisher and team – without whose help this book would have never been completed.

PREFACE

My journey to single motherhood started off humbly – a life that any one of you could be living now.

Having completed my journey, I now have the motivation and most importantly, the resources to tell my story. And, I want to tell my story in such a way that I can fulfill my long-awaited destiny of reaching out a helping hand to other single mothers.

The purpose of this book, in one way or another – is to give other single mothers a sense of **HOPE** in knowing the right direction to move from their current predicament to a fulfilling and happy life.

I have learnt, the hard way and by the gracious love of strangers (many who have become friends) many essential *survival skills* to being a Single Mother I would now like to give back to society, share my experiences of living in this Malaysian community, as a soon-to-be single parent and then finally as a single parent.

This book will be a *single reference point* that any single mother can tap into to seek the help needed – be it assistance to meet their basic essential requirements - from emotional help, to women rights' advocates and set up structures; all of which are being denied to so many single mothers, who so desperately need help and guidance.

Besides functioning as a **HOT LINE DIRECTORY** for women of all ages to contact in their hopeless moments, it is my vision that we can form a body of *sisterhood* in support of our daily needs; and all in persistent and consistent daily action for the grander dream of bringing about and living our best lives yet.

I truly believe that women of all ages can come together to help one another, to hold each others' hands and to tell each other that it is going to be alright, to just hang in there and to take one baby step at a time.

Lastly, my goal is to formulate and design a working social system that can help single mothers **STAND UP** tall and **STEP UP** to the call of life. I am eager to share this Nobel Prize winning programme *S.M.I.L.E HOME SYSTEMS©* (refer to Chapter 9) that is my dream to extend to women around the globe.

INTRODUCTION

A LIFE SENTENCE OF GREATNESS

Single motherhood is probably the toughest job in the world if you do it RIGHT. In fact, it precedes any job, as it is a *life sentence* that any woman with offspring(s) would have to bear.

As harsh as it may sound, the funnier and more realistic bunch of us will likely be nodding our heads in agreement to this *life sentence* tag; and you could either choose to embrace this reality with optimism, or let the *punishment* run and ruin your entire life. So which will it be? What are you going to choose to do?

For single mothers, or those who know that they are inevitably heading towards becoming one, the question to ask yourself is what do you want to experience out of this crazy mess that life seems to be putting you through?

Ask yourself what *taste* you would like to get out of this experience? A bitter one? Sour? Or sweet satisfaction? Know that the outcome is entirely up to YOU and the kind of choices that YOU make.

And reading this book would **ABSOLUTELY** change your life and help you make the **RIGHT CHOICES**.

Just imagine for a moment that five years from now, after reading this book and applying my **10 KEYS** which are my **SECRET SKILLS** by taking action towards living your **BEST LIFE FORWARD** – you will see that all your dreams will have come true. A nice house, financial security (or even financial freedom), experiencing a great journey in creating wonderful memories with your children, family and friends...and who knows, to find love again.

So just by picking up this book – give yourself a pat on the back – your wonderful journey has already begun!

Indeed you have made the right decision to take a turn for the better by reading, and by being informed, to take better action. In each Chapter, I will take you deeper into the heart of some of the biggest challenges faced by single mothers, and provide you with the answers to all those burning questions that you are too afraid to ask.

But here's an exemption clause: There are women who have made the right decision to take single motherhood by the horns and make the best out of it, and perhaps even to read this book. Yet, there are amongst these, those who still cannot grasp the concept and fully leveraging on the **SECRET SKILLS** learnt.

Some will probably take a much longer time to be truly enlightened on the ways to optimise their single motherhood status – I attribute this to the probability of a Higher Being who probably still thinks that the time is not now and has not readied these mothers, and perhaps they need more time and go through more life lessons in order to understand the **LAWS OF ATTRACTION** and the **LAW OF KARMA**.

But for all it's worth, on the reasons of being able to comprehend the 10 **SECRET SKILLS** that I am going to share, I'd say it revolves around the **BALANCE OF LIFE**. So though some will never be able to get out of the rut, so be it.

Do you know that single motherhood is not always about sob stories of hardship, betrayal, rudeness, neglect, sorrow and loneliness? As tough as its responsibilities and burdens are, single motherhood is a very common phase of life that an increasing number of women, in this modern age, are going through.

More important is that your happiness and everything you have ever wanted in your life or thought it ever could be - is right here. Right within your grasp and capabilities.

I'd like you to do a little experiment with me. Right now, at this very moment, put down this book you are reading. Close your eyes for a moment and give yourself a few minutes to clear your head of any distractions.

In the silence of your mind and imagination of your future possibilities – ask yourself if you can just *feel* it? Your happiness, your destiny, your ambition, your purpose in life is as near and as real as your mind allows it.

Not many women realise their great ability to being able to change their situation is actually in their thoughts and thinking. YOU, possess the most powerful thing to control your entire inner universe. It is sitting right between your ears – YOUR 3-pound brain. All that is required is that you unleash this mind power, and harness it for the right action.

Single motherhood life can be the most rewarding life a woman can ever experience. The way to score a perfect 10 (on your own scales!) in life is first by admitting that you are **NOT PERFECT**. No one in this world is PERFECT.

It doesn't matter what other people may say or try to influence you to do; most importantly you must **BELIEVE** in your own intuition and learn to ignore the negatives voices in your head. Learn to identify these negative thoughts, turn their *volume* down and finally learn and adopt a revolutionary proven system and *break* through in *life*.

Now let me start by sharing a little background about my previous life as a married woman.

It all started when I was 23 years old - too young to understand what the difference is between true love and marriage, and that they are two totally different things. In most parts of Asian culture, this is not something taught to us by our parents. I believe our parents did not know any better either, as the world is changing too fast revolutionising the way we work, interact and socialise. It is so different now from the days of our grandparents, when the males were perceived as predominant, the one to lead the family and be the breadwinner, and the women were to stay at home to care for the children and nurture the family. This is how we grew up, learning from the examples of our own parents and other close family units and friends. That is how we learn. We saw and observed, we thought that is how it should be when the time comes for us to get married and start a family.

I came from a very close-knit peaceful family of loving parents from various religious backgrounds and we respected and loved each other very much. I always dreamt of how wonderful it would be for me to be married and have lots of people around me who will care and love me unconditionally.

Unfortunately I was dead wrong. As my parents protected me the best way they knew how I didn't know early on that there are all sorts of people out there in the world who are very different. Some will even hurt you to get what they want, and not feel a single bit of remorse about what they have done. They may not feel guilty at all because they themselves were brought up in an environment in which they thought it is ok to do so. This is all they know themselves, because of what they saw and experienced in their own family environment. Some may grow up planning and thinking that they are going to do better, but in sad actual fact, they only repeat the same mistakes and end up hurting their loved ones.

In my case, the **LAW OF KARMA** continued into my married life at the time. Only after I got married and lived with my in-laws for a decade did I learn of my husband's abusive childhood. Only then did I begin to hear of the stories behind the very tragic life of my then husband and his family, and why my then husband behaved the way he did.

I do now think my in-laws feel some measure of remorse and regret and do try to make good with their grandchildren. Deep down, only he knows what kind of person he is and all the terrible things he has done to 'break' his own family and other close family members. Perhaps it is a little too late now, but I think he is finally beginning to realise what he has done to his own children and siblings.

I also came to find out and confirm of my husband's affair. He hadn't provided any financial support to me since the beginning of our relationship.

But my tipping point came when my then husband physically abused me in front of my children and his mother. That was when I finally put my foot down and took drastic action to leave the abusive environment and end my marriage.

After more than a decade, this cycle of horrible **KARMA** that they had unconsciously created two generations back was broken by the **CHOICE** I had the strength to finally make.

I did not want this cycle to continue into my children's future! It is important to plant the right seeds for my children and provide them with a safe and happy environment to grow up in even when it meant divorce for their parents. With this **CHANGE**, I had the **POWER** to place my kids in a different environment - a complete opposite to the abusive environment they had been experiencing for one decade.

Now, my children can see a fresh new perspective of how a loving environment should be and could be. To learn, to feel, to see, to experience for themselves that this is how a loving family should be. Even better, by experiencing and learning more profound knowledge from going through life challenging lessons, and by practising *GOOD DHARMA* - by believing in a higher power, that you are here in this world for a purpose.

Everything that has happened to you in life has served its purpose to teach us great life lessons. In return, when we are ready, we shall teach others what we have learnt so to benefit all beings and thereby turning the wheel of **KARMA** in a positive way and making this world a better place for all beings.

Now eight years on since my divorce, my children are happy and well-adjusted teenagers.

By **THE SECRET OF SHARING** as my story above, I have bestowed you with one of my best-kept secrets. Today if you will trust your own instincts, start by opening up yourself to your close friends and family members. Share with them that you wish to seek their help - if they are willing to listen – you do not have to feel depressed, beaten up, fearful or feel that nothing can be done in your current situation or that life is hopeless.

Enough of lies about your true potential! You shall no longer subscribe to that lie because **YOU ARE WORTH IT** and **YOU** have every **POWER** in your cells to be consciously making happy thoughts by merely practising *Good Dharma*.

If you are ready now, allow your thoughts to float away, then pick up your phone and call someone. Tell at least 20 people (don't ask me why, but 20 is a number that sounds intuitively congruent) that starting today, you want to be happy. Share with them your existing not-so-great situation and how you have vividly imagined yourself taking action to come out of it.

By changing your conscious thoughts of what **YOU** want in life instead of what you don't want, you will be on a revolutionary journey to a path of compassion, peace, warmth and happiness. Share with them what kind of help or assistance you need right now in order for you to get closer to your state of happiness and positive vision. Always remember to focus on the things that YOU want and not the things you do not want, and take baby steps to conquer your fear and tough challenges ahead. Get out from the negative state of mind and always remember to do the **RIGHT** thing. Later in this book I talk about what is the **RIGHT** thing to do or as I like to call it *big rock secrets*.

Chapter 1

SECRETS OF SHARING

KEY1: #Unlocking the Secrets in Life
KEY2: #Digging up the Long-Buried Dream
KEY3: #Opening up to Receiving

E very journey begins with a single step. Let me help you get on to the *freedom ship* and begin this tough journey with the fundamental starting point – **SHARING**.

This is the very FIRST KEY that this book provides you with; **THE KEY TO UNLOCKING THE SECRETS IN LIFE**. Share the real story of your life with at least 20 people and see what happens. Sounds foolish? As unconvincing as this may seem to you NOW, contact me after you've done so to let me know I was right all along. Sharing your story with others can be a real life-altering moment. Building those walls around you can only stunt your own growth. It is understandable that after the hell you've been through you feel afraid of being *exposed naked* by sharing your horrifying secrets, but by opening up to people you'll see that vulnerability can be also quite rewarding. Be honest and don't skip even the darkest details of your situation and life. Tell people where you've been and where you see yourself in the future and watch how the universe takes its turn.

Once you've dared to be genuine, magical doors will open and meaningful relationships will be created. You do not have to face this alone. There are millions of people walking in your shoes that can relate and be compassionate and understanding. Take it from me; the warrior who fought and won the very same battle.

Now, let me share with you MY personal story.

My name is **CJ Rose**. I was born in **1971** in a small town called Sitiawan, Perak, Malaysia. I grew up in a very traditional, down-to-earth family. We were not rich, but my parents had a steady flow of income that was enough to provide for my sister, and I.

Long story short, they did a great job raising us. **My father** was the one who was constantly spoiling me by showering me with toys, pets and everything a child could wish for, while my mother was in charge for instilling discipline and was encouraging me to go beyond the finish line I had drawn in my mind. I have her to thank for stepping out of my comfort zone to share these words with you.

Even though she wasn't too excited about me following my dream and pursuing art instead of applying at the local University, I have inherited my drawing talent from my mother, just as my sister is gifted in music like our father. You see, art and music are in our blood, but it was not our culture to embrace art and music. That's the reason my mother wasn't so fond of the idea of me being an artist. She always used to say how artists become famous only after their death, when their paintings are worth millions. I understand that now and what it is to be a mother, I mean. So protective of your children you only want what's best for them. That's what my mum was doing. She just wanted me to have a stable job with pension benefits, so that I'll be secured for the years that are yet to come.

But you cannot shut down a dream just like that, can you? Being so passionate about drawing, I have created a few unique pieces of my own. I would like to share with you all that I am now and all that I stand for through my masterpiece *D'VASE© by CJ Rose*

My Masterpiece.

The vivid and vibrant colours represent my heart and soul and they are cleverly packed in this magnificent, uniquely shaped vase that represent my body and mind. The humongous fish stands for the reflection of the wheel of life. The longer you stare at this remarkable masterpiece full-in-character, the more you begin to wonder about my spirit and you discover more about my life with each different perspective from which you are looking at.

I am sure that this exceptional drawing took the breath of those who understand and appreciate art. There's no doubt that I am gifted in art, but living a life filled with terror, I never really had a chance to pursue this dream of mine. It has always been and still is a dream of mine, to have a gallery in Tokyo, Paris and in New York by the time I am 60. There's still time! Check with me in 20 years to see how I am living my perfect life.

Speaking of dreams, I would like to share with you the SECOND KEY – **THE KEY TO DIG UP THE LONG-BURIED DREAM.** We all have dreams and wishes but playing the role of the abused wife in a horror movie called *our life*, has made us toss them away. But they aren't really gone. They never are. They are part of which we are - a centerpiece of our existence.

Now that you are finally free from the chains of a cruel marriage, **SHARE YOUR DREAMS** with people. Tell them what you've always wanted but never had the chance to pursue. Who knows, maybe one of those people can contribute to your dreams coming true. Maybe, perhaps, you can make that happen for someone. This is the THIRD KEY that I want to provide you - **THE KEY IN RECEIVING.** Sharing and receiving are two parts that must coexist. You cannot possibly expect to reach a helping hand after you've shared your story, if you do not listen to other people's problems. So, put aside your own and listen to someone else's story. This is not only the human thing to do, but just by listening to people's problems and imagining what others are going through will you better understand and realise that you are not alone. When facing such serious life hurdles, people usually lose touch with the rest of the world. Sharing and receiving will help you get through those hard times.

—— **CHAPTER 2** ——

SECRETS OF CHILDREN

KEY1: #Being Happy
KEY2: #Developing High Esteem
KEY3: #Encouraging Independence

B eing a mother is the most precious feeling in the world. Children enhance our lives so incredibly that there is absolutely nothing that can produce the joy that motherhood brings. This pure, unconditional love cannot be measured. It goes beyond everything. The need to protect our children becomes our sole purpose in life. They are the reason why women stay trapped in such horrible marriages. The things we endure for our children. But don't we know better than that? When I finally got the courage to turn a new leaf and get a divorce, I realized something. I realized that happiness couldn't be created but must be encouraged.

If I am ever granted a single wish, it will be for my children to live a happy life. You must be thinking how clichéd this is, as there is no parent that will wish differently, but trust me on this – you cannot make your children happy but we must be the best role models for them. You are your children best friend and in turn they look up to you. They cannot be happy if they watch you suffer day in and day out. That being said, the FIRST KEY to your child's happiness is **THE KEY FOR YOU TO BE HAPPY.** Seeing their mother truly happy, children will be encouraged to live life to the fullest. Now that you've finally met freedom, spread your wings and breathe the life in. Find happiness in the small things -- this is the first step towards your contribution to your child's happiness.

Life has been cruel. My days filled with fear and suffering, have kept me up most of the nights tossing and turning, and making master plans for starting over. Finally saying *"This is it, I've had enough"* was my most loyal companion through that petrifying experience. As if I had the courage. I deeply regret not doing it the very first time I saw him for the man he truly was. But the funny thing is, none of us now-single-once-married-and-abused mums do.

During this blissful journey of offering support to women who've gone through the same, I've learned that it wasn't just me. We were all scared to take matters into our own hands.

If you recognise yourself and have lived your married life trembling and scared, and have children, then you know that this traumatic experience for them is your number one enemy in the unsuccessful attempts to establish a healthy relationship with your children. Having spent years in an unhappy home, they refuse to see the beautiful side of life and only see the negative side of things. They lose their sense of how much they can truly achieve and set their goals pretty low, afraid of disappointment. You owe it to them, as you owe it to yourself to fill them with positive thoughts and encouragement.

This brings me to the SECOND KEY is **THE KEY IN DEVELOPING HIGH SELF-ESTEEM.** A healthy, high self-esteem is a child's shield that will protect him/her in facing life-battles, as well as the armor that will help them declare victory. Your job is to strike the iron while still hot, and help shape it beautifully.

On the request of many who have been seeking advice on ways to reconnect with your children after the years of being mistreated, I have decided to write and devote this chapter to you. This second key will open the door you've unintentionally closed and once you enter, you'll be step ahead to encouraging your children's happiness. My personal experience has shown me that with the following steps you can motivate your children and boost their self-esteem:

- Show them #UNCONDITIONALLOVE
- #BLESS and #PRAISE them
- #LISTEN to them in order to gain understanding
- Be REALISTIC -- part ways with unrealistic expectations
- SPEND #QUALITY and #FUNTIME together

Once your children develop a healthy self-esteem, they are ready for the world. Being prepared for the challenges that they will face in their life journey including failing and falling and being able to stand up again and try to do better. It is time for you to scoot over to the backseat and allow them to take the wheel in their hands.

The final and most important KEY that will allow you to enjoy your child's happiness is **THE KEY TO ENCOURAGE INDEPENDENCE.** You are no longer the goal-setter in their lives.

Now that you've done your job and geared your children up with self-confidence and ultimate love, it is time for you to step aside. You've guided them how to aim high, but only by staying out of their way can they achieve their grandiose dreams.

Having their backs, encouraging them to pursue their own purpose in life and being their personal positive encourager you've already put them on the path to greatness. It is now time for you to enjoy the ride and watch how they get there on their own, independent and without any limitations or high expectations from their mother.

Be careful, if you tell them your opinion too often, your well-intentioned advice can be easily mistaken for not being on board with the decisions they've made for themselves. Only by being moderate in your guidance you can truly enjoy the beauty of being the proud mother of happy and independent children.

Always bear in mind that no one is perfect. Do not blame yourself for not changing your life sooner if your children struggle to find their own ways. No one is flawless; so do not expect things to always go smoothly. Don't stress over your efforts to stop your children from making the same mistakes that you did; instead, guide them on how to overcome the obstacles they meet in life and be their support when they hit a wall.

Remember there is, **NO PATH TO HAPPINESS, HAPPINESS IS THE PATH**.

CHAPTER 3

SECRETS OF MINDSET & SPIRIT

KEY1: #Embarking on a Spiritual Journey
KEY2: #Turning Off the Voice of the World
KEY3: #Opening Up to Your Life Purposes

People easily get used to gliding through their own lives. They settle into their daily routines so quickly, as they are programmed to do so. They establish strict boundaries, even when they are perfectly aware that making changes is crucial in order for them to swim to the surface, when life has held them under water for so long.

If you are one of those people, it is time to take drastic measures. You may not believe me now, but only if you experience a state that is outside of your normal life, can you then only truly begin to challenge yourself. Sometimes it is completely necessary to head for a total change in the way you are living your life.

Those of us who have been victims of violence and abuse, in order to start standing on our own two feet again unafraid, we need to cleanse both our mind and spirit first.

The very FIRST KEY that can help you open the door that leads to finding your inner peace is **THE KEY TO EMBARK ON A SPIRITUAL JOURNEY.** While we're at it, I would like to share with you the spiritual encounter I had when I was just four years old. I remember it clearly as it was yesterday, this deep sense of my own existence. I was taking a nap in my bedroom when I had this out-of-body experience. I found myself floating in the air and a warm and blissful sensation suddenly took over me. I was floating over my kitchen and looking out in the living room with such blurred vision. It was then when I tried to move my hands and push myself when the miracle happened. I cannot describe that sensation of swimming in the air through words. When I finally got to my bedroom I was even more shocked to see my body lying in the bed. I landed gently and the next thing I remember was waking up. Even then I was fully aware that it was not just a dream. Today, I can still remember that pleasant feeling. Of course as a 4-year-old girl I wasn't really aware what had just happened, so I decided to keep it a secret. I haven't shared this with anyone for many years. A spiritual guru told me that I was given one of the most rare gifts.

You do not have to wait around for such an encounter to discover yourself. As I said, it is a rare gift indeed, and the reason why I have shared my spiritual journey with you is so you can take it as an example.

Embarking on a spiritual voyage can really help when you've experienced such a difficult life. It allows you to know how to overcome your limits, provides you with new perspectives and helps you gain an incredible mental clarity. By going into the depths of the things that are unknown, you will also define your relationship with yourself that will fill that missing piece in your puzzle of your life.

Only when out of your comfort zone, can you really embrace the things you never expected that can heighten and change your world. Just as spiritual clearness, having a balanced mindfulness plays a vital part in this new page of your life. The SECOND KEY is about your mindset and it is **THE KEY TO TURN OFF THE VOICE OF THE WORLD.** Being a victim of an abusive marriage I lost touch with the outside world. Living in a closed shell where only negative things happened, my overall life became negative. If you hear that you're worthless long enough, you will eventually start to believe it. Once I got rid of all the negativity in my life, I realized how peaceful, beautiful and extremely enjoyable life could be. You can do the same. Take the TV for example. A horror movie with the volume to zero is not scary at all. When you're watching a conversational talk show when the volume is on mute, your mind is at peace because you cannot hear all the disturbing statements that are being said. My point is – WHAT WE HEAR CAN REGULATE THE STATE OF OUR MIND. As Shakespeare said, *"Sound maketh a man – sound braketh a man"*. Make your inner voice be the strongest voice in your life that will guide you through your journey.

After making the biggest change in your life and deciding to start over, your must be wondering what's next. What should you do with your life? I know I was. I will not tell you that it won't be scary, because it will be. There will be times when you will feel lost and hopeless, as if you've flushed your whole life down the drain. But eventually you will learn how to stand strong. That is why you have me, to be your friend, your voice of reason and this book as your first source of support.

The THIRD KEY I want to offer you is **THE KEY TO OPEN UP TO THE PURPOSES IN YOUR LIFE.** Remember these words as this might be the best advice that has ever been offered to you. We are told that in order to succeed we must seize the day and take every opportunity, but the question is why don't we? How can we open ourselves after everything we've been through? It was quite a struggle, but I have made it. Now, I would like to share with you what kept me going and what helped me clear my mind and how I took advantage of the challenges that life has been throwing at me:

1. LET GO of the FEAR of making changes.
2. Always LISTEN to your INNER VOICE.
3. APPRAISE your own #HAPPINESS.
4. RECOGNISE when you are not fully fulfilled and do something about it.
5. LEARN how to take better care of yourself.
6. DWELL in life's possibilities.
7. DO WHAT YOU LOVE. Find what work satisfies you the most.
8. #LOVE your transformed self.

Open your mind and spirit to new adventures. Otherwise, how are you supposed to let go of the negative things and welcome all the wonderful things those that make you happy?

Chapter 4

SECRETS OF WELLNESS & BODY

KEY1: #Caring for Yourself
KEY2: #Staying Physically Active
KEY3: #Learning to Multitask

I love wellness. I mean, who doesn't? Achieving that state of emotional and physical well being, while living a happy and balanced life is something we all strive for. But what the wellness community fails to mention, is that our optimal well being feels very much out of reach for us single mothers.

I used to dream of being able to cross my legs and take a lotus position, close my eyes and have the time to closely observe my thoughts, breathe, and simply meditate. But almost every attempt of achieving a balanced state was a failure. I have two sons Li Hung (18), Hung Le (10), and a daughter Xiao Xing (14) -- a young adult, a boy and a teenage daughter. You can only imagine the level of their needs. From toddlers to teens, my house was always noisy. And as much as I love the sound of their hubbub, at times when I was struggling to meet a payment deadline, that noise used to release steam out of my ears. Pretty far from practicing yoga, don't you think? The reason I chose to write this chapter is fairly simple. The importance of the wellness skills is not to be neglected. Maybe I have learned it the hard way, but let me help you get on the right track.

It took me a pretty long time, and the road to becoming able to practice wellness was indeed bumpy. But now, in my 45th year of my life, I can finally say that I am happy. However, there were times when I used to stare the nervous breakdown in the face. From the moment I decided to leave my marriage, my role in this world was to find a way to raise my children the right way. I wasn't allowed to see my kids for a whole 9 months, and my youngest one was only 2 years old then. So where was the wellness then? Not even in the back of my mind. My point is to tell you that I know how hard it is. Truly. Your purpose in this world is nothing but watching your babies grow into healthy and responsible adults. But to do so, to really enjoy each and every moment of their happiness, you must also think of your own well-being.

The FIRST KEY is **THE KEY IN CARING FOR YOURSELF**. I know that it seems as though nobody understands what you are going through, but trust me I have been there. One paycheck and the inability to cover all expenses found a way to defeat my inner warrior, but the fact that my children had needed me to be my best version, made me pick up the shield and block my life's struggles. And the best version of myself has to feel good too. Watching my friends receive gifts and flowers from their husbands used to get to me, until I realized that I don't need anyone to make me feel special. To care for yourself means to treat yourself. Treat yourself with a body massage when you can afford it, or go to the sauna. Buy yourself something nice for some special occasion. Fill your vase with your favorite flowers, enjoy a soothing bubble bath, and do activities that will uplift your mood. You may wonder what this has to do with your physical shape, but I have realized that at those times that I actually felt good, I had also more energy and was in better physical shape. This key may not be your traditional wellness skill, but you are not a traditional woman. You are a single mum. Every single day of your life is beyond the ordinary.

The SECOND KEY is **THE KEY IN STAYING PHYSICALLY ACTIVE**. Being active physically is essential for maintaining your wellness. I have signed my kids up for many different activities throughout these past 8 years. From football to martial arts, I have really done my best to keep them active in what I could afford. As for me, I have my routines that keep my wellness in check. I enjoy morning walks and tread mill for 40 minutes that cleanse my inner worries, keeps me active and maintains my focus. You should do the same. Not necessarily the treadmill, but you have to find your own routine. Squeeze some physical activity in your busy days. I used to prolong this for as long as I could, until I found myself so exhausted that I could barely breathe. We all need to shake off our bad energy. It isn't impossible.

Here is a thought or two:

- Try getting off the bus a few stops before and spend some time walking before you get to work.
- Grab a ball and play a game with your kids.
- Wake up 10 minutes earlier and do morning exercises like sit ups or push ups.

- Enjoy an evening walk in the park.
- Dance to your favorite song.

Being a working single mother is not only overwhelming, but exhausting. There is so much to do and yet so little time. While trying to tackle problems here and there, I have come up with a technique – **THE KEY TO FILL TWO NEEDS WITH ONE DEED** or in short – multitasking. For instance, instead of cooking your kids dinner and worrying about the ridiculously enormous electricity bill that just came, try to help them with their homework. Beat the eggs and put your focus on their school papers. This will give you some extra minutes later that night that will be reserved just for you – a time to say OM and practice yoga. Try multitasking with all kinds of activities for one whole week, and see the improvements.

You don't need to spend money to remain healthy physically and emotionally. The power to choose to nurture wellness is within you. Get rid of your layers of worries and insecurities and you will find your ability to reach your overall well-being.

CHAPTER 5

SECRETS OF EMOTION

KEY1: #Taking a Break
KEY2: #Loving Yourself
KEY3: #Receiving Double the Love

S omeone once said, *"A man's work is from sun to sun, but a woman's work is never done."* Signing up for the toughest, but most precious 24/7 job in the world, and leaving your hopes and dreams behind, so you can give your children their best chance in this world, is to be deeply admired. But what if you don't have a man who works from sun to sun? Now that takes the motherhood challenge to a completely different level. It is just like walking on hot coal bare footed. There is no one to take over when your feet are burning, or to pass you some shoes for that matter. You are on your own. You are supposed to juggle everything, every day, fighting the dizziness and staying sane and strong for the children's sake.

The daunting challenge of being a single mother surely adds in extra weight, and the overweight burden you carry seems more than your fragile back can handle. Is that what you really think? Then, why are you still moving forward? Why hasn't the weight of your massive responsibilities cracked your spine already?

I used to feel just like you. Afraid that my burden will smash me like a bug. And the worst part is that we all want to believe the cliché 'the beginning is the hardest'. Well, news flash, it is not. It is just that – a beginning, and to begin something is easy as 1,2,3. Is beginning to run a marathon hard? No, it isn't; you start it after the ready, set, go. Having the strength to finish it though, now that is the tricky part. The same thing is with being a single mother. I was told how the first couple of months will be the hardest, and that after that, I will start doing everything on autopilot. Well, real life isn't that simple. Some things are so much easier said than done; this is one of them.

Single motherhood doesn't have a now and later. The flow of responsibilities is gradual, as your children grow, so does the level of your worries. Being on your own means that you don't have a reliable partner to consult with and you are the only one who pulls the strings and makes the decisions. Sometimes you will pull the wrong one and make a bad move – that is undeniable.

When that situation occurs, I want you to implement my **KEY IN GIVING YOURSELF A BREAK**. I used to beat myself up over the wrong choices I had made. The self-doubt of my decisions and the guilt over my not-so-bright judgments, have left some scars on my emotional self. But then I realized that I am only human, and as such, I am entitled to not having all the right answers all the time. Everybody falls and fails. If you surround yourself with women who are currently walking in your shoes, you will see how each of them is imperfect. The level of responsibilities as a single mother can push you over the edge of a cliff. But when you find yourself staring into a chasm, cry it out, wipe your tears, and find your way back again, because your children need you. And they see and cherish the sacrifice you make for them, so give yourself a break when you slip every once in a while.

Somewhere between rushing to work, running errands, doing chores and fixing meals, we forget that *we are also living a life*. Many of the women who contact me, fail to realize that they have lost touch with themselves, and that is demolishing them emotionally. Do not let your life pass you by. You may have been put on this earth to shape your children into becoming healthy, strong and confident adults, but you are also alive and need to find your own happiness.

So I want you to do something for me. Look yourself in the mirror and ask yourself: Who am I? What do I want? What does make ME happy? Write down your answers and take my **KEY TO LOVING YOURSELF**. Accept that you matter too, and find some time to do something you love every week. Whether it is reading, painting or playing a sport, make sure to squeeze some time for your passions and hobbies in your busy week, and enjoy yourself. When I feel the weight on my shoulders is weighing me down, I pour myself a nice glass of wine, trigger my creativity, and start drawing.

But, sometimes I forget that I am no superwoman. I am CJ Rose. An ordinary Malaysian woman, who is struggling to be both a mother and a father to my children, and doing my best to ensure that my children will have a good life – one in which I sacrificed everything to make happen. But, I get lost too and have found a way to overcome my hopelessness. When I finally stopped just *getting by*, I have started living my life much more *happily*. The feeling of hopelessness can start pulling bricks from your emotional wall. And if you do not want to wake up one day only to find yourself in emotional ruins, I suggest you to make my **KEY IN FEEDBACK – TWICE THE PARENT, DOUBLE THE LOVE**, a part of your day-to-day life. Always, but always, no matter what you do, no matter how you think you could have done something much better. No matter how low you feel, know that the fact that you are doing everything on your own shouldn't make you prone to depression, but a confidence-booster. You may be working for two, and loving your children for two, so you can fill the hole that the missing parent has made, but you have been also receiving for two. This might charge your batteries and give you strength for the new challenges that life has thrown at you. Always remember, your hands may be full, but so is your heart.

CHAPTER 6

SECRETS OF FINANCIAL SKILLS

KEY1: #Have a Budget
KEY2: #Be Smart About Grocery Shopping
KEY3: #Create Wealth

Have you recently taken a look at your wallet and asked yourself where is all that cash that I had just yesterday? And your pockets do not have holes, nor have you bought that amazing dress you had a glimpse of the other day. The problem with being a single mother is that unlike the two-parent families, you have on average 47% less monthly income. Talk about a financial struggle, right?

As a single mother, you are the one who should make sure that your children's needs are met. That includes rent/mortgage, food, education, clothes and all of the other hidden expenses that go hand-in-hand with children. That is only one way to stretching your budget, and that is by being diligent. Managing your income can be overwhelming, but it isn't impossible.

The first step towards getting the most out of every single dollar, is ensuring that your rent/mortgage fits in your budget. Ideally, it shouldn't be higher than 26% of your monthly income. If you have an option to move, in order to save money in the long haul, that is something that is definitely worth considering.

The sad and cruel truth, unfortunately, is that almost half of the divorced single mothers do not get child support. Living with one, modest source of income and a couple of bundles of joy running around the house is more than overwhelming. But even if that is the case, there is still a way to climb the stairs that lead towards financial independence. I know I did.

Even though the court ordered my ex-husband to pay MYR1,000.00 per month, nothing was forth coming. Eight years on now and I still haven't received a single cent from him.

Making the ends meet on my own, with three wonderful children, each of them with their own needs, was one hell of a scuffle. Forced to whittle the spending and make cuts here and there, I have come up with a solution that helped me get through the hard days, and now, I want to share my secret with you.

These are my three keys that opened the door to my financial stability:

THE KEY IN MAKING A BUDGET. The crucial thing you need most is a budget. In order for you to keep a track of what you spend your money on and to ensure that you will still have food on the table on the 30th day of every month, making a budget is a must. If you are not sure how to do it, you can find many resources online, as well as free templates for making a budget that can be of great assistance. The important thing is to write down all of the things you need to make payments for, such as rent, bills, food, school stuff, etc. Once you have created your budget, the next step is to stick to that amount.

THE KEY FOR SMART GROCERY SHOPPING. Not having a strict plan each time you enter a store can be a real budget drain. Chances are, items will be forgotten, things you don't need will be bought, and you will never be able to stick to the dollar amount for grocery shopping you have created in your budget list. In order to avoid all of that, I suggest you do the following:

- Make sure your budget for groceries is fair. We all want to spend as little as possible, but before you limit yourself to a certain sum, you need to ensure that it will cover enough monthly food for the whole family, as well as ensure proper nutrition.
- Make a menu for each day. I have found this to be extremely helpful. Put the kids to sleep, pour yourself a glass of wine, grab some paper and a pen, and create a menu for every single meal for one whole month. This has helped me not to spend more than the amount I have in mind. Do this at the end of each month.
- Buy food in bulk. Now that you know what you will need for the following month, the best idea is to purchase in bulk in order to pay less and save money. Potatoes, rice, beans, etc. are best purchased in dry bulk.
- Shop for groceries, once a month (or once a week if you receive a weekly paycheck). The point is to avoid frequent trips to

the supermarket and prevent yourself from being tempted to spend a little more on a couple of extras.

— Save coupons. Maybe there was a time when you saw no point in saving a couple of cents, but in the long haul, this habit can be extremely rewarding. For instance, if your kids want something you cannot afford, make a deal with them. Put each cent saved with coupons in a special box, and tell them that when you reach the amount they need, you will buy them that special thing they desire so badly. This was a life-saver for me. Besides the money we managed to save, this task has also encouraged my kids to spend their pocket allowances more rationally.

THE KEY IN CREATING WEALTH. Save. Save. Save. That is the only way you will make an investment that will build up your wealth. Every month, have a small amount transferred from your bank account directly to your savings account. You can do it automatically. Go to your bank and set up an auto-draft on your account, that will automatically allocate funds each month. In the beginning you can start with a small amount, and gradually increase the percentage. I greatly appreciate the automatic transfer, and the money I have managed to save this way.

Finally, the last tip I want to give you is to be grateful. Instead of beating yourself up each time you fail to make a payment on time, try to be grateful for those bills that you have actually managed to pay.

Chapter 7

SECRETS OF SINGLE PARENTING

KEY1: #Trusting your Inner-Self
KEY2: #Staying Calm
KEY3: #Being Creative

CHAPTER 7

SECRETS OF SINGLE PARENTING

As I mix salt, water and flour into dough to make Roti Canai for breakfast, I realize how three so simple ingredients can make something so delightful if you just combine them. Three things can surely create miracles when they join forces. And I don't mean only in the kitchen, but in life in general. Think about it. What do you need from a relationship? Love, commitment and respect. What do you need to be truly happy? Purpose in life, love, and family.

So if you think that you have somehow wandered and reached the borderline to becoming a lousy parent and there is no way back, you are so wrong. I have been where you are standing right now. The fear of losing your children is indescribable. It spreads like a disease and eats you alive, until you are no longer able to breathe. But even when it seems that your life is nothing but pitch black, the spark can still be reignited. I can help you make the U-turn, and bring you back to where you once were. Even if you are the sole carrier of the burden, you can still be an outstanding parent.

My next three keys have created miracles for me, and they can do the same for you. Start implementing them today, to improve your parenting skills and be an awesome mum.

THE KEY IN TRUSTING YOUR INNER SELF. The most important thing I have learned on my journey of dealing with everything on my own, is to always TRUST my INSTINCTS. It may seem like a cliché, but only your heart knows what to do best. Being alone, and in charge from the simple everyday things many take for granted like what to wear for school, to the major struggle of making ends meet and extending the budget that it is simply never enough, can easily turn on the *low disk space* sign in your brain. We tend to over-think how to overcome the obstacle that come in our way and that usually clouds our judgment. What seemed like the right thing to do at first, can easily be ignored. That is why it is always important to trust your heart. You may be surprised by how strong your inner self is. So whenever you need to push your children's boundaries a little bit further, forbid electronic devices, make them study harder, or explain to them why their friend isn't the one they should be hanging with, always search for the answer inside of you. A mother's heart always knows best, so make sure to give it a little bit more credit.

THE KEY IN STAYING CALM. Trust me when I tell you that I know exactly how nerve-wrecking single motherhood can be. Busy days at work, a pile of unpaid bills lying around your house, fixing meals, cleaning after every meal, cleaning the house, getting the kids ready for school, picking them up, etc. can deprive you of many things you may wish to include in your life. Combine that with a couple of needy teenagers or hyperactive toddlers scribbling on the wall, and you may have a nervous breakdown. What I have learned so far is that one of the keys to being a good parent is having the ability to be calm. Remember that the way you feel when your child is testing your patience is not triggered by that event. If you replay your day in your mind, you will most likely find many other stress-triggers that have contributed for you to be so intolerant, and you will realize that snapping at your child will not solve a thing; it will only make things worst.

I have burned myself a couple of times before I finally realized that only by using my calm voice I can make my toddlers listen to me. Now, they are 18, 14 and 10 years old, so I am faced with different kind of problems, but I always use the same approach to solving them.

THE KEY IN BEING CREATIVE. A friend once said to me *"Being a single mother is an art"*. It certainly can be. Sometimes it feels like only the *talented* ones can make it. When you have so much to do, and there is so little time, you must find a different way to make things work for you. I am a really innovative person, so maybe that is the reason why I have managed to succeed so far, but I know in my heart that anyone can do it if they search for some hint of creativity inside of them. Being a single parent, means that sometimes you will have to choose your imagination over anything else, in order for you to satisfy everyone's needs. To be honest, there are still times when I feel my life is one big race. Like I am constantly on the track, rushing to the finish line, trying to complete all of the daily tasks. But life is unpredictable. It often throws at us more obligations that we think we are able to manage. And since you have children, you probably already have a ton of those.

So how can being creative give you the time to fulfil all of the tasks that are required from you as a parent? I usually involve the kids more. When they were little, I used to make a contest for washing dishes, cleaning their rooms, and other chores. That way my kids learnt the importance of doing something valuable with their free time, and we had more time to do something together as a family, whether it was working on some of their school projects or playing a game.

I believe that these three keys have shaped me into the mum my children deserve. I really hope that you can make my keys a part of your life, so you too can boost your skills as a single mother. I would love for you to contact me and share your experiences.

CHAPTER 8

SECRETS OF PREVENTION & DATING SKILLS

KEY1: #Trust your Judgement
KEY2: #Be Patient
KEY3: #Understand your Children's Feelings

The dating world is full of twists and turns. Should you pay attention to every word that comes to your mind, praying that the other party will find you fun, or simply be yourself? Should you wait for her/him to call, or is it better to leave a message? We have all been through these sweet complications more than once in our lives and we know how it goes. But, dating in a group, now that is like boiling the ocean.

You might be imagining what it is like for single parents in the dating zone, but you had no idea it is so down right difficult. How to pass the dating point and make your date flourish into a steady relationship? How to find a balance between being a mummy and being a partner without letting the first part overpower the other?

Now, I may not be able to help you find the right one, or make prince charming magically appear on his white horse, but as someone who has managed to find the successful formula for dating while being a single mother of three, I think that makes me more than qualified to provide you with three keys that will help you in your quest of finding the right person without scaring him off with your obligations.

THE KEY IN TRUSTING YOUR JUDGEMENT. When it comes to dating, whether you are a single mother or a 20 year old without a care in the world, the most important part is to always trust your judgment. If you feel like there is something off with your suitor and potential partner, then it is best to end it before it goes any further. You don't need that in your life, especially not when you have children to think about. Sometimes we get so disappointed in life, so we start grasping at straws. After a couple of failed relationships, sometimes a single nice word is enough to cloud your judgment. But, you know better than that. If you are not fully satisfied with her/his qualities, part your ways before you find yourself stuck in a bad relationship again.

THE KEY IN BEING PATIENT. When you find someone enjoyable, a match that really suits your needs, it surely feels like a breath of fresh air in your knotty and messy life. There is someone waiting to see you, someone who is trying to make you happy. This wonderful change is enough to make anyone want to dive in too fast. If you believe that the relationship has a long-term potential, it really won't hurt anyone to slow things up a bit, don't you agree? Patience is the fundamental quality that can award you with a healthy relationship. Here are some things you need to put on pause, until you are sure that the timing will not hurt anyone:

–   Do not get intimate too fast. You may think waiting to become sexually intimate is not something that a stable, grown up man would do, but that is not true. Try to get to know the person before you make such a connection, since you may be only blinded by the fact that you only crave the company. If your potential partner is serious about his intentions, she/he will appreciate your wishes to prolong intimacy, and will see it as a sign that you are willing to commit to the relationship.

–   Wait before you make introductions. Introducing the person you are dating to your kids, before you are absolutely sure about the nature of your relationship is a lethal mistake. Once you make the introductions, there is no going back, so make sure that it will only happen with the right person. I assume you are not in for some family drama that can result in tragedy, right?

–   Do not assign to her/him parenting roles too soon. Sometimes being the single parent and having so many errands to do can be exhausting, so we cannot wait to involve the other person. Avoid this for as long as possible, until you get to that stage when you will be absolutely sure that she/he loves helping you out. And no, even if picking up that birthday cake is on his way, that is not something you should ask him to do. At least not yet.

THE KEY IN UNDERSTANDING CHILDREN'S FEELINGS. Once you make the introductions, you can expect all kinds of reactions. Sometimes your kids can be cold and mean, and sometimes they will find a way to use certain situations to get what they want. Do not be too harsh on them as they are simply expressing resistance. Usually, the main culprit for their behaviour is the fact that you were entirely theirs, and now all of a sudden, they get to share you with another person. Even if your new partner is the best person in the world, they will most likely behave the same way. Instead of panicking or judging their actions, try to take a more understanding approach.

– Tell your kids that you love them more than anything in the world and that nothing or no one will ever change that.
– Explain to them that having fun is as much as important to you as it is to them, and spending time with your new partner is fun to you.
– Talk to them about their fears. Let them know that you understand that they fear your family will not be the same. Explain to them why they have nothing to worry about.
– Take it slow. Your kids may need more time to accept the fact that you now again have another person in your life. Just work with how they react in the moment.
– Don't worry. Eventually they will get used to the idea and accept your situation. After all, everyone including your children will recognise how happy your new partner makes you. And that is what every child wants its mother to be, happy. Once you have both sides satisfied, you will see the beauty of it. That, I guarantee.

CHAPTER 9

SECRETS OF S.M.I.L.E HOME SYSTEMS

Years of abuse can surely crush your spirit. You begin to feel as if you are trapped inside a maze, and the exit is nowhere to be found. You get used to terror of that life, and eventually accept it as normal. But when they separate you from the thing you cherish the most - your children, your inner mamma bear wakes up, and so the roar begins. At least, that is what happened to me.

After 10 years of being treated like a *doormat* by my ex-husband, I made a conscious decision to leave. I was left on the street, with no money, no car, and no one to turn to (my parents lived far away from where I was). So you can only imagine the thoughts that were circling in my head. I was prevented form getting my personal belongings. But the worst was being forced to live without my children for 9 months. That happened 8 years ago, when my youngest was only 2 years old.

Although it took me a while to stand firmly on the ground, thanks to the bear inside of me that they had poked, I became stronger than ever, and I knew that moment would shape my entire future. And so, it did. I managed to win the fight and take my children with me.

Homeless, devastated, crushed, I have surely learned a lot from that dark period of my life. That is why I can relate to all those women who are going through such hard times. That is why I will fight with my last breath, to ensure that those women who are victims of violent marriages find security again.

But I cannot do this alone. I need the help of all other mama bears from all over the world to accomplish it. Although it is still work in progress, I know that my *S.M.I.L.E HOME SYSTEMS*© will help those in need.

> *S.M.I.L.E* stands for:
> *S*ingle
> *M*other
> *I*ntermediate
> *L*earning
> *E*ducation

So you must be wondering what ***S.M.I.L.E HOME SYSTEMS*** is all about? It is a halfway home to single mothers who want to escape their violent and awful life and ensure a better future for their children.

If there had been such a place when I was kicked out, I would not have felt so alone. I would have felt safe and secure, and I would have been fueled by confidence, instead of struggling to kick the suicidal thoughts out of my head.

The idea is to provide single mothers and their children with a *temporary* home, until they are ready to get back on their feet and prepare them to accept life's challenges as strong and independent women and mothers. So, here is my idea of the ***S.M.I.L.E HOME SYSTEMS***:

My goal is to raise RM1.8 million, to fund the very first ***S.M.I.L.E HOME SYSTEMS*** home. First, in Seremban 2 (where I live), then to expand throughout Malaysia, and ultimately to spread this programme on a global scale. The house will not only be a place for the women to sleep. It will also be their home and most importantly their safe haven.

Each home would accommodate 5 single mothers and their children. The idea is that 2 of the mums go to work and 3 of them (those women who either have no skills or qualifications, or are scared due to the abuse) will stay at home. One mum will cook and ensure that the other members are provided with a hot meal at all times, one will be in charge of cleaning the house and ensuring that they live in a clean and sanitary environment, and the third mum will go grocery shopping, do errands and make sure that they all have what they need. Of course, the working mums will be the main backbone of the group and provide financial support for school stuff, household items, entertainment, insurance, and all of the things the members of that home need to live a normal life.

The ***S.M.I.L.E HOMES ORG*** will cover the monthly expenses needed for running the household. The women living in the ***S.M.I.L.E HOMES*** will be taught new skills and capabilities, that will not only make them more qualified for different jobs, but also boost their self confidence and *train* them to become independent and self-sufficient women. This will enable them to regain their strength and start their own home. They will be taught skills that will enable them to get involved in any of the following:

- Health Care (Both Mentally and Physically)
- Child Care and Babysitting
- Finance and Investing
- Home Base Businesses and Job Opportunities
- Creating New Home Base Jobs
- Online Businesses
- Driving (think Uber and Grabcar)
- Organic Gardening
- Cleaners (Home and Office)

The members of the *S.M.I.L.E HOME SYSTEMS* would live as a family, following set rules and other regulations that will ensure they maintain their normal function as a happy family unit. This noble-prize-winning grand idea is that the family stays together for at least five years, or until the children are independent enough.

To ensure the children's normal development there will be personal development programmes, and they will also be given scholarships. The kids will attend a school that is nearby their halfway home, and will not be deprived of the things their friends at school have. Clean clothes, school equipment, food, a safe home and a place where they can learn and grow into smart and independent adults will all be a part of their life.

These *S.M.I.L.E HOMES* kids, after becoming self-supporting individuals, will then contribute back to the community and help us set up another *S.M.I.L.E HOMES*. The kids from every *S.M.I.L.E HOMES* will do the same, so this single mum shelter will become available for any woman in need all over the country.

If you find this idea as amazing as I think it is, please make a donation to fund the *S.M.I.L.E HOME SYSTEMS* and let's together help those single mothers. They really do need it.

CHAPTER 10

MY FINAL ADVISE

As difficult as life as a single mum is, it can also be very empowering. It wasn't the life I had planned or chose but because I was left with no choice my three children and I moved forward to grasp what life had to offer. We didn't change overnight, it has been a long journey but we grew with each new step. Our scars are still deep but it is those scars that have shaped us into who we are today.

I want to leave you with my ultimate single mum survival kit.

My single mum survival kit No.1 – #TrustInGod

God was there and God still is. He gave me the ultimate blessings – my three children and he gave us all strength and calmed our fears.

My single mum survival kit No.2 – #PowerToChange

Always remember that it is NOT OK to get abused. If it happens once it can happen again. And so you need to take action immediately and move forward if you have ever been abused, even just once. Never stay for the sake of your children because remember your children learn from their parents experiences. If they see dad beating up mum they will grow up thinking it is acceptable for men to beat women and that it is the correct way of being and perfect environment they should be living. They will carry this same behaviour into their adult lives and only land up hurting their own families in time to come.

My single mum survival kit No.3 – #DealingWithFear

Step up your game and learn to deal with the monster called fear. When you become a single mum your life suddenly turns upside down. It seems that fear can become as much a part of life as breathing. I was afraid to start the next day because of what might happen.

Fear can be overwhelming and if we let it, fear can consume us and be the monster under the bed.

My single mum survival kit No.4 - #DailyAffirmations

Start each new day with affirmations; they work wonders. I am a great believer and use them to kick start my day, no matter how I otherwise feel.

As Buddha said: ***you become what you believe***. And the only way this can happen is for you to reinforce the connection between your unconscious mind and your conscious mind with daily affirmations. This will make you more resilient when faced with difficult and challenging circumstances.

To start your day on the right foot, so that your body follows your mind and together you can face any kind of day, do this as soon as you open your eyes every morning.

Lay flat on your back and breathe for 2 minutes. Then start to whisper the following affirmations to yourself. Repeat each one 3 times.

"I AM #EXCITEDABOUTTODAY".
"IT IS GOING TO BE AN #INCREDIBLEDAY".
"I AM #HAPPY"
"I AM #HEALTHY"
"I AM #WEALTHY"
"I AM #SECURE"
"I AM #WORTHY"
"I AM #POSITIVE"
"I AM #ABUNDANTLYBLESSED"
"I AM #GRATEFUL"
"I AM #BEAUTIFUL"
"I AM #CONFIDENT"
"I AM #COURAGEOUS"

Cultivate this process as your daily ritual until it becomes a habit. Affirmations pack a powerful punch and are sure-fire ways to kick start your perfect day on the right foot.

Finally, I'm here to tell you that divorce is not the end of the road. My marriage bent, cracked, and finally broke. It isn't easy, and it's not what you have chosen, but you will learn to live again and be happy.

It doesn't matter what life cards you are dealt with; it just matters how you play them. It's up to YOU to determine your destiny, and don't let anyone tell you otherwise.

When it was first happening there seemed to be no light at the end of the tunnel. Single motherhood has allowed me to discover things about myself I'd never had the opportunity to find out when I was married: I am independent and accomplished, and I am able to run a household, bring home a paycheck, and take excellent care of my children.

Having come out stronger and learnt to be happy again I am here to tell you: There is **HELP**, there is **HOPE**, there is **HEALING**.

If you continue to be persistent, sooner or later you'll succeed. You just have to make sure you learn from your mistakes along the way.

During my journey of single motherhood I worked smart and learnt new skills together with my kids. I taught my kids and myself to invest in growing my passive income assets (now worth millions) by signing up for **KC Lau's PREMIUM WEBMINAR MEMBERSHIP (PWM) Programme.**

So here are my **TOP THREE SECRETS** to becoming a successful working single mum:

1) **Always LOVE YOURSELF more** - take care of your health and dress smart when meeting with clients.

2) **Manage YOUR TIME** effectively and efficiently - do what's important first by prioritising your family needs and work requirements. Find your balance - have your personal fun time and quiet time and build it into our daily routine.

3) **Learn NEW SKILLS** - take action to earn more money progressively, save even more to reinvest in financial tools that generate PASSIVE INCOME without having to trade your time for money. All successful people take massive action to learn and apply new skills in financial education. As Rich Dad

Poor Dad said our school system would never teach us to be financially savvy and free from the rat race.

And most importantly, always remember to spend your money wisely.

"To accomplish great things, we must not only act, but also dream; not only plan, but also believe," Anatole France.

CHAPTER 11

LOOKING BACK ON IT NOW

L ife After the Heartbreak of Divorce and the promise of HOPE beyond the pain -- Surviving and Thriving as a Single Mum

You married your soul mate or so you thought but it's now over! Whatever your story what is important, once the relationship you entered with so much hope and dreams is official dissolved, is figuring out what you want as a newly single person, how that life is going to pan out and how you take that next step to start moving in that direction.

This chapter is dedicated to some of my friends who have been brave to share their stories of how they turned lemons into lemonade.

There are many divorce success stories. I don't know the ratio of divorce success stories versus non-successes, but I do know that there is light at the end of the tunnel. These single mothers, all carrying wounds, but all offer insight, wisdom, and encouragement. The lessons include listening for God's higher calling, holding your head high, daring to dream again and championing your children.

LING Yin / 34 / 1 son - 13 years / Widow

"I started really living 10 years ago after the death of my husband. I had been married for 3 years and had a 3 year old son when he passed away. However, I was not happy in my relationship and it also wasn't a good one.

Had he not passed away our relationship would have nevertheless ended in divorce. My late husband, 17 years my senior, was possessive and didn't allow me to work. He didn't give me any allowance, so I had to dip into my savings to care for and support my son while we were staying with my in-laws. That taught me to never depend on a man for financial support.

After his death, I moved out from my in-laws place and left my son in their care during the weekdays while I worked. I only saw my son on the weekends. I will never forget that whenever it was time for him to go back to his grandparents place he would cry as if the world had come to an end. That broke my heart each and every time. This living arrangement went on every weekend for almost 2 years!

At the age of 23, I managed to start working an Administration job and at 29 had worked my way up to become a HR Manager, which I am till today.

While I was lucky to have had the support of my family and friends during the hard times; I also knew I had to do things differently and make a change for the sake of my son.

My son was understandably very badly affected by the death of his father. He faced many social issues – bullying, was and still is an introvert and very quiet. I changed his school to a private kindergarten and brought him back to live with me and care for him even during the week while I still continued to work full-time. I also at the same time started night classes in mass communications and a business degree; both of which I completed within 3.5 years!

I was also inspired to try out different businesses in travel, health and beauty as well as network marketing. Attending various business seminars has really been an eye opener for me. Through networking I have come to realize that people have been programmed to work hard and make money. However, many fail to realize that it has taken away a huge chunk of time from loved ones and the things they are passionate about. As the saying goes, the rich will always get richer, and that is because they make money work hard for them. Especially during this economic instability, we all need a Plan B.

I got retrenched earlier this year due to downsizing, but with the right attitude and mindset I was quickly able to climb back on my feet again and get back in the game.

I am now happy with work, in my new relationship for the past 10 years and most importantly I am thriving and surviving as a single mother.

The past has thought me many lessons and helps remind me not to go back to the old life. I have also learnt not to be dependent on men. As women we need to be strong and independent especially financially. It is when you take charge of your life that your children will also respect you and look up to you as their role model.

I hope that my story will be an inspiration to other women to pursue your passion while young and energetic. Do not live regretting that you did not enjoy life. Remember, fear is all in your head."

Ling's Tips:

1. Don't be afraid to learn new things.
2. Talk about your situation to anyone. You will be surprised at what new ideas come about.
3. Talk also to people in similar situations as yours. They will be able to empathise, understand and support you. You will not feel alone.
4. Women must be financially independent. Do not rely on your partner to provide for you and your children.
5. For your first pot of gold, INVEST wisely not greedily.
6. Never be afraid to leave a bad relationship for a better future. No one deserves to be treated badly. This applies to bad bosses as well!
7. Women can do things that men can too. In fact, even more!

Genji Lee / 55 / 2 children - 1 daughter aged 32 & 1 son aged 30 / 26 years Divorced

"My ex-husband was the jealous and possessive type. He constantly jumped to conclusions and made many accusations and didn't understand my job demands as a hotelier. The straw that broke the camel's back was when he physically abused me that one time. I didn't believe in second chances; not after physical abuse. I strongly believe that if a man can be violent even once; he will do it again. And I didn't want to go on with the relationship with 'for my children's sake', which are what many women would do.

So I ran away and took my children with me. I was blessed to have my parents help in looking after my children while I continued to work as a hotelier. But it was still tough being a single parent. I had to be both the mother and father to my daughter and son who were

6 and 4 years old respectively at the time I left my then husband. I also had to single handedly provide financially for them and also look after my parents.

To add to the pressure, my then husband dragged out the divorce for 10 years. That took a toll on my children and me.

My children are now adults and look after me very well and also often take me on holidays. My son still stays with me and has asked me to retire and enjoy life not working but I am still undecided if I should carry on till 60. My hope is that he will find a good woman and marry soon. My daughter is married and has given me a grandson. My days are now filled with joy and laughter. I am also now happily remarried."

Genji's Tips:

1. There is no one who is perfect. But its necessary to ensure your life partner is a good person with a good heart. Looks and money don't matter.
2. Women must not put up with violence and physical abuse from a man under any circumstances. Get out of an abusive relationship immediately and get help from family, friends and community support.

TASHA Edmunds / 2 children -14 year old daughter & 12 year old son / 3 years Divorced

"My single motherhood began 3.5 years ago when I had to move back to KL after living my married life in Singapore for one year. I was married for 14 years.

The first six months was extremely tough. I had to juggle so many things at the same time and started work again after a one-year break to provide for my two children and I also had to deal with my mother's terminal illness.

I lost my mother one year later. On hindsight starting over in KL was a good thing as I was able to spend her last year with her. Had I still been living in Singapore I would not have had any time with her before her passing. So I continue to feel blessed in many ways.

I took up a self-motivation course to help me put things in perspective and get through the initial changes to my life and cope with the challenges that came long with it. With time, everything got easier and I learnt to be happy again.

My children are now well adjusted, very grounded and at peace. Even friends and family have recognized how they have grown as individuals and have matured. As for me, I have grown as a person and am in a much happier place. Most of all I have embraced my new independence.

It was important to me that my children still have a connection with their father. So he is able to come by my house to be with the kids whenever he is in KL. We even still do 'family' things like meals and outings."

Tasha's Tips:

1. When the going gets tough, the tough get going! But, trust me, there is always a light at the end of the tunnel. Life will get better.
2. We need to stay strong, especially when you have others dependent on you, even though it may seem as the whole world is crashing down on you.
3. God will provide. My faith is strong and has been a big part of my continuous achievements as a single mother.

JASMINE / 35 / 2 daughters - aged 11 & 8 years / Widow (married for 11 years)
"My husband, passed away in a hospital two years ago having succumbed to dengue after being hospitalized for 1 week. My girls did not see their father while he was in hospital for the last week of his life but only for a few minutes in the hospital before he breathed his last breath. It left us all devastated.

I was left with nothing. My late husband was a salesman but had no house, no savings, no EPF or SOCSO. Whatever little savings we had was used for his medical expenses. It has been and still is very tough as a single parent but I know I need to go on living for the sake of my children.

After my husband passed on, I went back to live in my parents house, and my brother, who works in Singapore, has been very generous in helping me out financially. He has been providing for my parents as well as my daughters and me. He paid for my car and has been taking care of all living expenses for my parents, daughters and me.

I own a small home-based business baking and selling cookies and cakes, which I have been doing for the last seven years. I also take on small online projects for Simply Cookies - a social enterprise that trains single mothers how to bake – creating posters and marketing materials. I want to become a successful business woman.

All my paychecks from my business and other part-time jobs are put aside as savings for my daughters' education. Their education is my top priority now. They have been performing top of their year (not just class) in school and that makes me extremely proud.

I am proud to say that my daughters are mature beyond their ages and understand the financial constrains we have trying to make ends meet. So, if they ask for something and the budget doesn't allow for it, I will tell them it will have to wait till we have the money; and they understand. They do not kick up a tantrum. I am very blessed to have such wonderful children. They are even so intuitive to know that talking about my husband still makes me sad and will always change the topic immediately.

My daughters' happiness is my utmost importance. I am not interested in another relationship despite family pressuring me to remarry. My sole focus is my children and their education.

Being a single mother has not been easy. It's the toughest job to take care of my children without a husband having to do everything from A to Z single-handedly. I know with time life will get easier."

Jasmine's Tips:

1. Don't give up on life.
2. Make your main purpose the education of your children. Nothing is more important than a good education.
3. Work hard and DO NOT depend on others.

Elaine / 34 / 3 boys – aged 16, 14 & 12 / 5 years Divorced

"I was married for 10 years before I decided to call it quits. Prior to ending my marriage I already started building up funds and had mentally prepared myself for divorce.

I was financially independent even during my marriage, working in the hospitality industry. However when my marriage ended the hardest part for me was that I had 'lost' my eldest son who was brainwashed by his father. While I had my two younger boys with me all the time, I made it a point to ensure that my eldest son (even till now) is with me during the any holidays. To make matters more difficult, my mother, whom I had to move in with during the divorce process, made things more difficult by accusing me of not caring for my children whenever I came back from work late. But in actual fact I was working overtime to earn more money for my boys and me.

I now work full time at Simply Cookies - social enterprise that empowers single mothers to be mothers and career women at the same time – baking cookies as well as managing 7 retail outlets. My boys and I are now happy again."

Elaine's Tips:

1. Be strong and prepare yourself for single life.
2. Ensure you are knowledgeable in all aspects of life from knowledge about everything, to financial independence and being emotionally strong.
3. Financial Independence is of utmost importance.

CHAPTER 12

DIVORCE 101

Tips and advice in preparing for a divorce and its process. What you need to know when marriages begin to fail and are beyond repair, whom to turn to for advice and support?

This chapter is intended to help make the challenges and stress that come with a divorce that much easier. It provides a basic understanding of and general information on the Malaysian Family Law.

This is NOT intended as legal advise and should NOT be taken as legal advise. Consult a family lawyer for legal redress and a support group for emotional support.

DIVORCE Q&A

In Malaysia, there are two types of divorce of marriage for non-Muslims:

1) Divorce by mutual consent (both parties agree to the divorce) and
2) Divorce without mutual consent

DIVORCE BY MUTUAL CONSENT (JOINT PETITION)

Both parties to the marriage can jointly file a divorce where they can mutually agree to divorce.

By a joint petition, both parties can freely decide on the maintenance for wife and children, custody and care of the children, division of matrimonial assets.

DIVORCE WITHOUT MUTUAL CONSENT (UNILATERAL/ SINGLE PETITION)

Either party to a marriage may file a petition to divorce without consent of the other party, on the grounds that the marriage has broken down.

The breakdown of the marriage can be grounded one of the reasons as follows:

1) that the other party has committed adultery;

2) that the other party has behaved in such a way that it cannot reasonably be expected to live together;
3) that the other party has deserted for a continuous period of at least 2 years; OR
4) that the parties to the marriage have lived apart for a continuous period of at least 2 years.

One common misconception is that the parties to the marriage must be living apart for more than 2 years before a divorce can be filed. The reality is that if both parties agree to divorce, they DO NOT have to be living separately.

Living apart for more than 2 years is merely a reason to file for single petition divorce. There are many other reasons to file for divorce as mentioned above.

WHO HAS THE RIGHT OVER THE CUSTODY OF THE CHILDREN?

In a joint petition, both parties can mutually agree to propose any arrangement for the children, including joint custody after divorce.

In a single petition, either party can make an application for the custodianship.

The court will decide the custodianship after considering all factors including:

1) The welfare of the children
2) The wishes of the parents
3) The wishes of the child if the child is eligible to express an independent opinion.

There is a rebuttable presumption that the custodianship of a child below 7 years belongs to the mother. This is a presumption which is rebuttable by the father.

WHO HAS THE RIGHT & INTEREST OVER MATRIMONIAL PROPERTY?

In a joint petition, both parties can mutually agree to propose any arrangement in relation to the property.

In a single petition, either party can make application for the division of matrimonial property.

If the property is acquired by the sole effort of the party, the court may divide the property as the court thinks reasonable. The party upon whose effort the assets were acquired will receive a greater proportion. If the property is acquired by joint effort, the court may divide the property as the court thinks reasonable after considering factors like the extent of the contributions (both financial and non-financial) made by each party.

WIFE & CHILDREN'S MAINTENANCE

Wife's and children's maintenance has to be identified separately in a divorce petition.

In a joint petition, both parties can mutually agree to propose any arrangement for the maintenance.

In a single petition, either party can make application for the maintenance and ancillary relief.

The court will decide after considering all factors including:

1) the needs of the wife and children
2) the living standard of the parties during marriage
3) the income of the parties.

HOW LONG DOES IT TAKE FOR A DIVORCE MATTER TO BE COMPLETED?

The actual time needed may vary in each and every single case depending on the following factors:

1) The date of hearing granted by the court (whether it is early or late)

2) The complexity of the case
3) The time needed for both parties to reach a settlement (for joint petition's case)
4) The appointed lawyer's efficiency.

Generally, a joint petition divorce matter takes 5 to 6 months to be completed while a unilateral petition divorce (without mutual consent) takes longer. The divorce matter could take more time if it is contested.

WHAT IS THE BRIEF & GENERAL PROCEDURE FOR JOINT PETITION TO DIVORCE?

1) Consult a lawyer. If you need help to find one email wecare. askme@gmail.com
2) With your lawyer's advice, discuss and make settlement with your spouse for the arrangement of children, property & maintenance (if any).
3) Sign the divorce petition and related documents prepared by your lawyer.
4) Wait for the hearing date after the filing of your application in the High Court.
5) Attend the hearing with your lawyer. If you or your spouse cannot attend the hearing, refer to your lawyer for solutions.
6) Obtain the divorce certificate three months after a divorce order is granted by the judge.

NOTE:

1) Parties do not need to attend any NRD tribunal for joint petition to divorce.
2) Parties do not need to be separated for 2 years before a joint petition to divorce can be filed.
3) Parties do not need to specify the reason for divorce in joint petition.

WHO SHOULD BEAR THE LEGAL FEE? HUSBAND OR WIFE?

For a joint petition matter, there are two options:

1) Either party pay for the whole legal fee OR
2) Both parties share the legal fee in a proportion that is mutually agreed.

For single petition matter, each party has to bear their own legal fees.

HOW MUCH IS THE LEGAL FEES?

Generally, a joint petition's legal fee is cheaper than a single petition's (without mutual consent).

The legal fee chargeable varies from one case to another depending on the following factors:

1) The complexity of the case as it affects the amount of time and skill a lawyer requires;
2) The complexity of the Petition's Divorce Arrangement & Settlement;
3) Whether or not the divorce petition is contested. Legal fee for contested matter is generally higher than uncontested matter.

OTHER FAQS:

FOREIGN MARRIAGE/ DIVORCE

Q: I am a foreigner in Malaysia who has registered my marriage overseas. Can I file for a divorce here?
A: Yes, if you are residing in Malaysia even if your marriage is not registered in Malaysia.

Q: I am a Malaysian who is residing overseas now. Can I file for a divorce in Malaysia?

A: Yes, you can sign the divorce documents overseas, and engage a lawyer to file your divorce in Malaysia.

Q: I am a Malaysian who had registered my marriage in Malaysia or at the Embassy of Malaysia. I have obtained a divorce certificate from overseas, but is my divorce certificate recognized in Malaysia?
A: No. Your overseas divorce certificate is not recognized in Malaysia. You need to engage a lawyer to apply for local court's declaration to give legal effect to your overseas divorce certificate, and update your marital status with the National Registration Department.

TWO YEARS SEPARATION REQUIREMENT
Q: Can I file for divorce within 2 years of my marriage?
A: Yes. It's possible.

Q: Do I need to separate with my spouse for 2 years before a divorce can be filed?
A: No, not necessary.

Q: Do I get 'automatic' divorce when I have separated with my spouse for more than 2 years?
A: No. You will still need to apply for the divorce in court.

NATIONAL REGISTRATION DEPARTMENT (NRD)
Q: Can I get a divorce by applying to the NRD without engaging a lawyer?
A: No.

Q: I have attended NRD's tribunal 3 times, am I considered divorced?
A: No. You need to engage a lawyer to proceed with a divorce.

Q: My divorce certificate is granted overseas. Can I submit the divorce certificate to NRD to update my marital status?
A: No. Your overseas divorce certificate is not recognised in Malaysia. You need to engage a lawyer to apply for local court's declaration to

give legal effect to your overseas divorce certificate, and update your marital status with NRD.

SPOUSE'S ISSUES

Q: My spouse refuses to divorce. Can I still file for a divorce?
A: Yes.

Q: My spouse refuses to sign any divorce document. Can I still file for a divorce?
A: Yes.

Q: I have lost the contact of my spouse/ my spouse has gone missing. Can I still file for a divorce?
A: Yes.

Q: My spouse is residing overseas now. Can I still file for a divorce?
A: Yes.

ANNULMENT

Q: What is annulment of marriage? Can I file for annulment?
A: Annulment is a legal procedure for declaring a marriage null and void. Consult your lawyer for more information.
 Source: http://www.mylawyer.com.my/article/divorce.php

FRAMEWORK OF FAMILY LAW IN MALAYSIA

1. INTRODUCTION

The very existence of family law is premised upon the fundamental right of a man and a woman to get married to form a family. Such a right is guaranteed by Article 12 of the Federal Constitution of Malaysia.

Whilst family law seems to connote only applications to persons who is related by blood or marriage, it is pertinent to note that it also applicable in some others relations, such as co-habitants, adopted parent and children.

It remains that in Malaysia there are two types of family law, one being the Syariah family law that applies to Muslims and the other being the civil family law that applies to non-Muslims.

The Syariah family law has long been in existent in Malaysia even prior to the civil family law when Muslims marry according to the various states Syariah law.

It is the objective of this chapter to provide some basic understanding of the civil division of the family law that governs non-Muslims and some sources for legal redress which are available for some cases.

2. RELEVANT ACTS OF PARLIAMENTS OR STATUTES AND THEIR PURPOSE

It cannot be said that it is the social, emotional and sentimental needs of every relationship formed that calls for the recognition and protection of rights amongst the parties.

2.1 Law Reform (Divorce and Marriages) Act 1976 ("LRA")

The LRA is a set of family laws that governs the civil marriage in our country. It laid down the laws on marriage and divorce and other matters auxiliary thereto, for example, maintenance of spouse and children, division of matrimonial property and child custody.

2.1.1 Marriage

The LRA became law on 1st March 1982 and provides for all marriage to be registered in order for it to be regarded as a valid marriage. Therefore any marriage which is not registered (for example amongst girlfriend and boyfriend and cohabitants) shall be regarded as invalid, thus have no protection whatsoever afforded under the family law context.

Having said that, all marriages that was not registered but solemnised under any law, religion or customary rites prior to 1st March 1982 are still legal marriages, thus valid so long as parties can show proof of solemnisation of their marriage such as certification or eye witnesses or better still, video recording.

It is further spelt out in the LRA that bigamy is disallowed under the law.

The LRA applies to all persons in Malaysia and to all persons domiciled in Malaysia but resident outside Malaysia. For this purposes, a person who is a citizen of Malaysia is deemed to be domiciled in Malaysia until the contrary is proven.

2.1.2 Divorce

For any marriage registered under the LRA, the Court shall have the power to grant a decree for divorce upon petition of one party to the marriage and such decree shall notwithstanding any written law to the contrary, be valid against the other party, notwithstanding the other party has converted to Islam.

There can be 4 grounds for a party to petition for divorce as follows, provided always that 2 years shall have expired at the time of petitioning from the date of the marriage:-

(a) Where one party to a marriage has converted to Islam;

(b) Where husband and wife mutually agreed that their marriage should be dissolved after expiration of two years from the date of their marriage by presenting a joint petition;

(c) Where there is breakdown of marriage which is provable by showing:-

   (i) either party had committed adultery;

   (ii) either party behaved in such a way that the petitioner cannot reasonably be expected to live together;

   (iii) the respondent has deserted the petitioner for a continuous period of at least 2 years; or

   (iv) the parties have lived apart for a continuous period of 2 years.

(d) Presumption of the other party to a marriage is death after seven years of continuous absence.

The LRA also provides that for divorce under the sole ground of irretrievable broken down of marriage, the petitioner must first refer their matrimonial difficulties to the Marriage Tribunal or Conciliatory Body at the National Registration Department (www.jpn.gov.my), which is established under the purview of the Ministry of Home Affairs, in order to obtain the relevant certification of whether the marriage can be reconciled.

In any divorce proceedings, regards shall have for the following auxiliary matters to be resolved.

Maintenance of Spouse (a.k.a Alimony)

The Court is empowered to award maintenance to a spouse even during the course of the divorce proceeding before a decree for divorce is granted.

Maintenance can be either paid from the husband to the wife or vice versa. It is the law that the assessment of maintenance shall base primarily on the "means and needs" of the parties for the purpose of continuing their standard of living such that during the subsistence of the marriage.

Such amount of maintenance awarded is regardless of the proportion that such maintenance bears to the income of the husband or wife, but having regard to the responsibility which the court apportions to each party for the breakdown of the marriage.

Maintenance of Children

Maintenance of children is essentially the obligation of both parents. However, judicial precedents inclined towards holding that the husband has the primary obligation to maintain the children whereas the mother has secondary obligation.

The law also states that the term maintenance should be construed widely as it signifies any form of material provision that will enable the wife and children to be placed in a position to enjoy the same standard of living as they did during the subsistence of the marriage.

Property Division

The inherent power of the court to order property division should be exercised judiciously in the pretext of safeguarding the benefit of the spouses but also the dependent children. This involves assets that are used jointly and severally for the benefit of the family as a whole. The principles for property division, on one hand, emphasize towards equality of division considering the needs of the minor children

On the other hand, the Court is mindful of the need to balance of whether the assets were acquired jointly or by the single effort of one party where in the latter case, the division cannot be based on the equality principle.

Custody of Children

As a general rule, there is a rebuttable presumption that it is for the good of a child below the age of 7 years to be with his or her mother but in deciding whether that presumption applies to the facts of any particular case, the court shall have regard to the undesirability of disturbing the life of a child by changes of custody from the father.

The court may at any time by order place a child in the custody of his or her father or mother, or where there are exceptional circumstances making it undesirable that the child be entrusted to either parent, of any other relative of the child or of any association the objects of which include child welfare or to any other suitable person.

Where there are two or more children of a marriage, the court shall not be bound to place both or all in the custody of the same person but shall consider the welfare of each independently.

In deciding in whose custody a child should be placed the paramount consideration shall be the welfare of the child and subject to this the court shall have regard to the wishes of the parents of the child; and to the wishes of the child, where he or she is of an age to express an independent opinion.

2.1.3 Judicial Separation

If 2 years have not been expired from the date of the marriage for purpose of petitioning for divorce, parties may consider the option to petition for judicial separation on the same 4 grounds as petition for divorce.

Judicial separation, once granted, allows parties to live apart and end their marital obligations but parties shall remain married until divorce. Such decree, if successfully obtained, will be useful for the winning party as a means of presenting a marriage offence leading to breakdown of marriage and with a view to applying for a divorce later.

Likewise, there are auxiliary matters to be resolved as in paragraph 2.1.2 above.

2.1.4 Nullity

A party can present a petition for nullity if the marriage is a void or voidable marriage which is the result of the absence of one of the requisites of a valid marriage, for example age (less than 21 years old), mental and physical capacity be incapable of contracting the marriage.

Other common grounds on which the marriage will be voidable are either party to the marriage did not validly consent to it; or the marriage had not been consummated owing to the incapacity or willful refusal of either party to the marriage which facts shall be ascertained by the Court.

2.2 Domestic Violence Act 1994

This Act was enacted to protect battered woman and children both physically and verbally. It became law on 1 June 1996.

Domestic violence is a crime and it is taken to have been committed if there is information tantamount to the commission of a related offence under the Penal Code. Notwithstanding that, many see it as a domestic or family affair which battered women defer in looking for help.

When this happens, the victim can:

1) First, seek immediate medical attention at the nearest Government Hospital (remember to always get your medical report out) immediately;
2) The victim or anyone close to the victim may make a report to the District Social Welfare Department (contact can be obtained at www.jkm.gov.my) or to the police; and
3) Inform the Social Welfare officer or the police if you need Interim Protection Order (which is valid for 12 months and can be renewed for a further 12 months) pending investigation and they will assist to obtain such order in court which will entails such necessary order to keep the victim safe. At this juncture, victims can voice out their concerns to the officers in charge, for instance any imminent physical abuse or threat in order for necessary arrangements to be made;

Should the offender officially be charged after investigation, victim may apply for Protection Order instead.

If the victim feels not convinced by the authority be in handling their case, they may have a lawyer hold a watching brief in court they have been subpoenaed to attend to give evidence against the spouse.

2.3 Guardianship of Infants Act 1961

The present Act deals primarily with the appointment of a guardian to a child's person and property. It also spells out the custody, rights and liabilities of the guardian of infants as well as provisions in regards to the control and management of the infants property until they attain the age of majority at 21 years.

2.4 Adoption Act 1952

A child under the age of 18 can be adopted by any person or couple who is 25 years old and above whom must not be less than 21 years older than the infant.

The latter requirement may be waived by the court if adopter is a relative or a mother of the child as the adopter can also a person who married the natural parent of the child.

An adoption order will be, made by the court only if it is satisfied that the consent of the parent or guardian of the child or the person liable to contribute to the support of the child has been obtained; or, that the adoption is in the best interest of the child.

2.5 Legitimacy Act 1961

An illegitimate child refers to him/her born out of wedlock, it is the purpose of this Act to provide for legitimation of a person by subsequent marriage of his/her parents.

2.6 Child Act 2001

This is basically the law that gives protection of child's right in Malaysia. As seen in the preamble of the Act.

This is an Act to consolidate and amend the laws relating to the care, protection and rehabilitation of children and to provide for matters connected therewith and incidental thereto.

Source: http://chiaassociates.com/
framework-of-family-law-in-malaysia/

Chapter 13

RESOURCES & COMMUNITY SUPPORT

M alaysian Single Mothers must first realise that they DO NOT have to struggle alone. Any single mother who needs help can check out organisations such as Jabatan Kebajikan, or even groups on Facebook here and here. There are even NGOs like one called Jumble Station (JS).

This chapter provides some useful links and contact information:

3.1 Government Departments

3.1.1 Ministry of Women, Family and Community Development
No 55, Persiaran Perdana Presint 4,
62100 Wilayah Persekutuan Putrajaya. Malaysia
Website: http://www.kpwkm.gov.my/

3.1.2 National Registration Department
Ministry of Home Affair
Marriage Tribunal or Conciliatory Body
No 20, Persiaran Perdana, Presint 2
Pusat Pentadbiran Kerajaan Persekutuan
62551 Wilayah Persekutuan Putrajaya. Malaysia
Website: http://www.jpn.gov.my/

3.1.3 Social Welfare Department
Ministry of Women, Family and Community Development
No 55, Persiaran Perdana Presint 4,
62100 Wilayah Persekutuan Putrajaya. Malaysia
Website: http://www.jkm.gov.my/

3.2 Non-Govermental Organisations (NGOs)

3.2.1 Woman's Aid Organization (WAO)
Assists women in crisis from all walks of life in a friendly, personal and supportive environment.
Website: http://www.wao.org.my/

3.2.2 The All Women's Action Society (AWAM)
Assists women in crisis from all walks of life in a friendly, personal and supportive environment.
Website: http://www.awam.org.my/

3.2.3 Sisters In Islam (SIS)
Promotes rights of women in Islam.
Website: http://www.sistersinislam.org.my/

3.2.4 Tenaganita (Woman's Force)
Promotess and protects the rights of womeb workers and migrant workers in a globalised world.
Website: http://www.humantrafficking.org/organizations/175

3.2.5 Kuala Lumpur Legal Aid Centre
Assits and delivers services to the disadvantaged, marginalised and truly deserving.
Website: http://www.kllac.com/

3.2.6 Jumble Station (JS)
Social entrepreneurship set up to empower Single Parents in need.
Email: jumblestation@gmail.com
Website: www.jumblestation1.blogspot.com

3.2.7 Simply Cookies
Social enterprise to empower single mothers to be financially independent by providing training (to bake) and employing single mother's to work alongside their children.
1-2-3, Block I, Persiaran Wawasan Setiawalk
47160 Puchong, Selangor
Tel: +60.3.5879.9642
Email: sue@simplycookies.asia
Website: www.simplycookies.asia

3.2.8 Befrienders Malaysia
For emotional support and public education
Hotline: 03-79568144 or 03-79568145
E-mail: sam@befrienders.org.my
Visit: 95 Jalan Templer, 46000, Petaling Jaya

4. Legal Advisor
Chia & Associates, Advocate & Solicitor
Mr. Chia Swee Yik
Address: A-2-20 Block A, Megan Phoenix,
Jalan 2/142A, Off Jalan Cheras, 56000 Kuala Lumpur
Mobile: +60.16.214.8218
Email: sweeyikchia@gmail.com
URL: www.chiaassociates.com

5. Online Financial Educator
KC Lau - The No.1 online financial blogger, educator and author and the best in Malaysia and South East Asia who offers a Premium Webminar Membership (PWM) Programme.
KCLau Dot Com Sdn Bhd
Address: No. 1-3, Jalan Solaris 2, Solaris Mont Kiara,
50480 Kuala Lumpur
Email: support@kclau.com

For all KC Lau's Money Tips and Financial Matters visit:
Webinar: https://kclau.com/webinar/ask-question/
Blog: https://**kclau**.com/
LinkedIn: https://my.linkedin.com/in/**kclau**
Facebook: https://www.facebook.com/**kclau**money/
YouTube: http://YouTube.com/KCLauMoney
Twitter: http://twitter.com/MoneyTips

Printed in the United States
By Bookmasters